Table of Contents

Written by Daniel Ho
Guitar performed and recorded by Daniel Ho
NCX2000 guitar photos by YAMAHA Guitars

Edited by Dean Pitchford
Photography by Lydia Miyashiro-Ho
Published by Daniel Ho Creations

ISBN: 0-9842928-4-5

EAN: 978-0-9842928-4-4

Foreword

I first met Daniel Ho in early 2009 when he came to The GRAMMY Museum® to perform with Tia Carrere for what was to become an annual staple of the week before the GRAMMY® Awards show, "Hawaii Night at the GRAMMY Museum®." Far before I knew what a successful artist and producer he was, I was struck by the effect his music had over the entire audience. When the first chords to "The Breakfast Song (Pineapple Mango)" were strummed, spontaneous dancing broke out in our Sound Stage. Whether of Hawaiian decent or not, people relate to Daniel's music.

Open-String Fingerstyle Method for Guitar is a perfect combination of simplistic teaching methods and intelligent musicality that makes mastering the basic concept of open-string technique enjoyable for students of any age and musical ability. Daniel's enthusiasm for his craft and ability to adjust lessons and exercises to both beginners and seasoned players makes it easy to start at any level—whether that be learning the parts of the guitar or jumping into the exercises with a new, open-string approach.

Daniel's knowledge of guitar along with his abilities as an artist and producer combine to make these lessons not only achievable, but enjoyable. He teaches you the basics and then gently pushes you forward by using repetitive chord exercises, necessary in grasping the fingering technique. As a beginning guitar player myself, this book has taught me, with one finger on my left hand, how to start playing the guitar. Enjoy!

Kait Stuebner - *Education Manager, The GRAMMY Museum®*

Daniel Ho's *Open-String Fingerstyle Method for Guitar* is more than a beginner's guide. It is a model on how to approach learning, and enjoying, any instrument. Starting with an introduction that Socrates would love, Daniel poses the question and then answers how best to learn to play the guitar and make music!

As we have come to expect from his books, he offers a clear and logical path from holding the guitar to performing standard voicings, open-string fingerstyle voicings, and exercises in various keys. To move the student to the next level, he concludes the book with information on transposing and the use of the G Kilauea tuning—a tuning system based on his years of composing and performing. This book is integrated with exercises, musical examples, and a CD that allows you to tune your guitar, hear examples of voicings, and even play along with the examples.

It is an outstanding work that could only be written by an accomplished musician, composer, and music educator!

William Doyle, DMA - *Professor of Music, El Camino College, Ars Nova Sinfonia*

The Question

What is the easiest possible way to play fingerstyle guitar?

I found the need to address this question in two settings: live performances and clinics.

Concerts can be as long as two hours, so playing bar chords and other chords that require fretting many strings can be strenuous. To reduce the pressure exerted by my left hand, I came up with easier voicings—ones that use more open strings.

As a guitar clinician, I am often asked to present 60 to 90 minute seminars on fingerstyle playing, demonstrating how accessible and easy it is. I focus my presentations on the basic essentials required to get "up-and-playing" quickly and with ease. By the end of each session, I try to leave the participants with enough knowledge to play simple songs in one key. By imparting this sense of accomplishment, I hope to inspire students to continue studying this wonderfully engaging instrument.

The Answer

Drawing on my experiences as a player and clinician, I evaluated various aspects of fingerstyle playing and worked to simplify the challenging elements of this technique. After careful analysis, I discovered a common denominator for all my findings: open strings.

Open strings are unfretted (or untouched) by the left hand. They are the essence of guitar playing for a number of reasons:

• A guitar sounds most resonant when the full lengths of the strings are vibrating.

• Open strings contribute to sympathetic vibrations and overtones that are not as prominent when strings are shortened by fretting with the left hand.

• When the left hand is not required to finger many notes, it is free to execute other parts.

• The sustained tone of open strings helps to smooth chord transitions.

The Lessons

This book and its accompanying audio CD introduce the *Open-String Fingerstyle Method*, an innovative concept that distinguishes open strings as the core principle of fingerstyle playing.

Starting with how to hold a guitar, we will go on to cover left and right hand fingerstyle techniques; modified voicings of the six definitive chords in each of the five most common guitar keys; and transpositions to other keys using a capo.

Also included are comprehensive exercises to get you playing fingerstyle right away!

About the Guitar

track
1 - 6

Guitars are generally classified into two main categories: acoustic and electric, i.e., those that can be heard unaided and those that require amplification. There are three types of acoustic guitars: classical, steel string, and archtop. Of those, the classical guitar is best suited for fingerstyle playing. The neck is a little wider and the nylon strings are spaced farther apart. This allows a guitarist to play individual strings with less interference from adjacent strings. Traditionally, the six strings of a guitar are tuned to E, A, D, G, B, and E—from the lowest pitched string to the highest. (Tracks 1 – 6 on the audio CD are reference pitches that will help you tune your instrument.) The picture below indicates the basic parts of a classical guitar.

Technique

Before getting into the musical aspects of fingerstyle playing, let's go over basic technique. It is extremely important to develop good playing habits from the start. Otherwise, practicing actually trains you to play inefficiently, and the resulting limitations will prove frustrating. It takes far more effort and time to undo bad habits and to re-learn good ones. The techniques presented in this book are classical guitar methods which provide a solid foundation for fingerstyle playing.

Holding the Guitar

Classical Position

Pictured to the left is the classical playing position. The guitar is placed between the legs with the waist of the guitar resting on the left leg. There are four points of contact—the right leg, left leg, chest, and right forearm—that keep the instrument stable and allow the left hand to move freely around the neck.

Casual Position

A more casual way of holding the guitar is to rest the waist of the guitar on the right leg. This position offers only three points of contact—the right leg, chest, and right forearm—which requires the left hand to control some of the horizontal movement of the instrument. With the exception of classical guitarists, most players favor this posture.

Left Hand Technique

• The fingernails on your left hand should be as short as possible, preferably no longer than your fingertips.

• Use the tips of your fingers to depress the strings. Keep your fingers curved, as they have more strength and leverage this way.

• Always keep your fingers as close to the fretboard as possible. Try not to let them stray high above the fretboard or curl under the neck.

• The thumb should press against the back of the neck opposite the other fingers, creating a counter-pressure. It should not be held to the side or over the top of the neck.

The following are examples of good left hand technique:

Here are examples of inefficient left hand technique:

Not using fingertip

Fingers too high

Pinky under neck

Fingers too high

Thumb over neck

8

Right Hand Technique

In classical technique the thumb, index, middle, and ring fingers are used to pluck the strings. The pinky is not used because it does not have as much strength or control as the other fingers.

The left sides of the fingernails glance the strings at a slight diagonal—the index, middle, and ring fingers pluck up toward the right forearm, and the thumb plucks down toward the right. Picking this way generates a smooth, full attack and a warm tone.

To produce a clear and balanced tone, pluck the strings over or around the sound hole. Plucking closer to the fretboard results in a darker tone with less attack; plucking near the bridge creates a bright sound with a strong midrange and sharp attack.

Resting Position

The resting position is a "home base" for the right hand. The flesh of the playing fingers rests on top of the strings. The fingernails touch the sides of the strings, ready to pluck them. Touching the strings allows you to feel where you are on the instrument without looking down at your hand.

Rest Strokes

There are two primary plucking techniques: rest strokes and free strokes. A rest stroke is performed by plucking a string, then allowing your finger to rest on the adjacent string. This technique creates a loud, rich tone without "fret buzz" because the string vibrates parallel to the fretboard. Rest strokes are used to feature melodies and solos—passages that require greater volume and presence.

Pluck string with index finger

Rest index finger on adjacent string

The same principle shown above applies to the middle and ring fingers.

Below is an example of a rest stroke using the thumb.

Pluck string with thumb

Rest thumb on adjacent string

Free Strokes

A free stroke is executed by plucking a string and not allowing your finger to rest on the adjacent string. This technique is used for faster passages or arpeggios, when all the strings should resonate simultaneously.

Pluck string with index finger

Do not rest index finger on adjacent string

The same principle shown above applies to the middle and ring fingers.

Below is an example of a free stroke using the thumb.

Pluck string with thumb

Do not rest thumb on adjacent string

Written Music

There are many ways in which music can be written. Contemporary guitar music is generally presented as chord symbols, chord graphs, tablature, or a combination thereof.

Fingers & Strings

Classical guitar notation uses numbers to identify which fingers on the left hand should be used to fret strings: 1 = index finger, 2 = middle finger, 3 = ring finger, and 4 = pinky. The letters *p, i, m,* and *a* are used to designate which fingers on the right hand should be used to pluck strings. The letters are abbreviations of Spanish words: *p = pulgar* (thumb), *i = indice* (index finger), *m = medio* (middle finger), and *a = anular* (ring finger). The pinky is not used, so it is not assigned a letter.

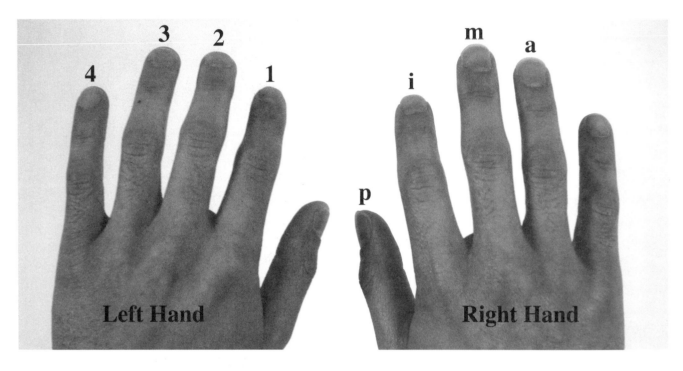

Left Hand   Right Hand

Guitar strings are identified with numbers:

6 = low E string
5 = A
4 = D
3 = G
2 = B
1 = high E string

In guitar music, these numbers appear in circles. The images on either side show the strings of a guitar and their corresponding numbers.

E A D G B E
6 5 4 3 2 1

E A D G B E
6 5 4 3 2 1

The finger and string information explained on the previous page will appear directly above or below the note to which it pertains. The following is an example of how they are used:

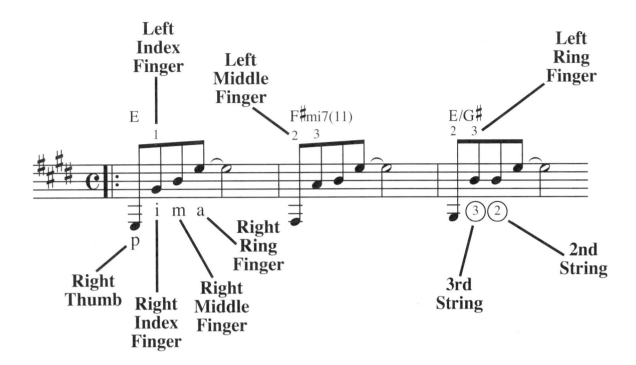

Tablature

How to read music notation will not be covered in this book, as it is quite involved. I have included it for guitarists who already know how to read. The tablature written below the notation is considerably more intuitive for the beginner.

Each of the six horizontal lines represents a string on the guitar. The letters to the left of the lines denote the string. The number written on a line indicates which fret on that string to finger with your left hand. 0 means to pluck the open string, 1 means to finger the first fret (the fret closest to the nut), 2 means to finger the second fret, and so on.

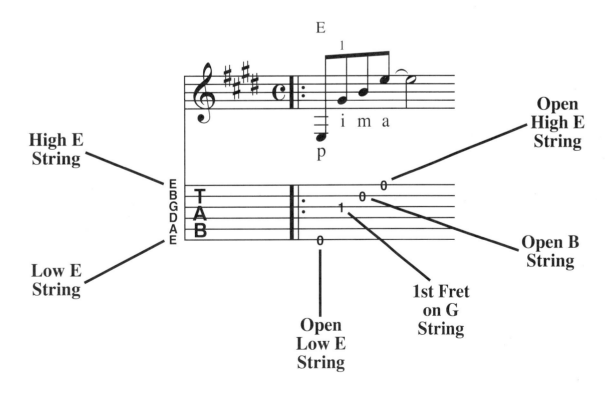

Chord Graphs

A chord graph is used to specify a particular voicing of a chord. It usually appears directly below a chord symbol and above the music staff.

• The vertical line to the far left represents the low E string (string number 6). The vertical line to the right of the low E string is A (string 5), the next is D (string 4), then G (string 3), then B (string 2), and the far right string is the high E string (string 1).

• A thick horizontal line at the top of the graph represents the nut of the guitar. The horizontal lines below it are frets.

• If the top line is not thicker than the rest of the lines, there will be a number followed by "fr." to the right of the graph. The number designates that fret as the top fret of the graph.

• An empty circle above the top line means to play the open string directly below it.

• An X above the top line means the string directly below it should not be played.

• A black dot on a vertical line means to finger that fret with your left hand.

• A curved line joining two dots means to hold all the strings down between and including those two dots with one finger—usually the index finger. This is called a bar.

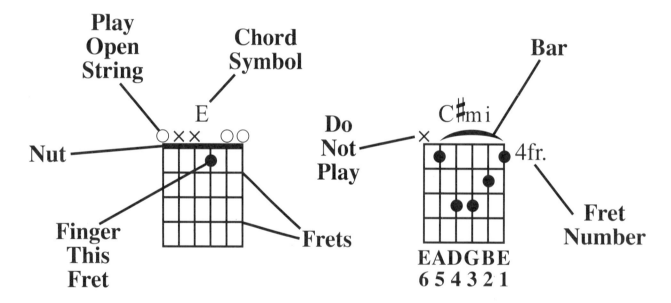

Concept to Fruition

This page outlines the set of parameters I used to develop the *Open-String Fingerstyle Method.*
It's as easy as 3, 4, 5, 6!

Three Fingers per Chord

Every voicing in the *Open-String Fingerstyle Method* can be played with three or fewer fingers on your left hand. Most of the voicings use only one or two fingers. One voicing of the E minor chord, as a matter of fact, is played entirely on open strings and requires no fretting by the left hand.

Four Fingers for *Four* Strings

Though fingerstyle playing requires more finesse from your right hand than strumming, it is actually easier on your left hand. When playing fingerstyle, the left hand isn't required to finger entire chord voicings; it is only accountable for the strings plucked by your right hand.

Because classical technique uses four fingers on the right hand to pluck strings, I have developed special voicings that only use four strings to define chords. Each finger on the right hand is assigned to a string, so no finger has to pluck more than one string.

To further simplify this method, these modified voicings utilize as many open strings as possible, easing the responsibilities of the left hand. Believe it or not, you can play all the main chords in the keys of E and G, using only two fingers on your left hand!

Five Common Guitar Keys

A key is the tonal center of a piece of music. The five keys most often used in guitar music are E, A, D, G, and C. Why? You guessed it—because these keys use the greatest number of open strings!

Six Main Chords

The main chords of a key are based on the first six notes of a key's scale. A scale is made up of seven notes, but the seventh note forms a different kind of chord that we don't need to know right now. The scale determines whether a chord is major or minor. For instance, chords built on the first, fourth and fifth notes of a scale are always major, and chords built on the second, third and sixth notes of a scale are always minor. This is important to remember because it will help you figure out whether a chord in a particular key is major or minor. Below is a chart of the six main chords in the keys of E, A, D, G, and C.

	Key of E	Key of A	Key of D	Key of G	Key of C
1 - major chord	E	A	D	G	C
2 - minor chord	F#mi	Bmi	Emi	Ami	Dmi
3 - minor chord	G#mi	C#mi	F#mi	Bmi	Emi
4 - major chord	A	D	G	C	F
5 - major chord	B	E	A	D	G
6 - minor chord	C#mi	F#mi	Bmi	Emi	Ami

Key of E
Standard Guitar Voicings

The following chord graphs are standard guitar voicings of the six main chords in the key of E.

track 7

E	F#mi	G#mi	A	B7	C#mi

    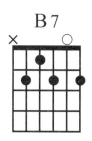 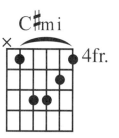

Most beginners are taught these voicings early on, but the strength and agility required to finger many notes or bar chords with the left hand is often discouraging. So I have devised alternate voicings.

Open-String Fingerstyle Voicings

The chord graphs below are special voicings that can be used in place of the standard guitar voicings seen directly above each chord. I created these voicings to make fingerstyle playing as easy as possible. They maximize the number of open strings and limit the number of strings played to four.

Notice that some of the chord symbols are modified versions of the standard chords. This is because I have customized the open-string fingerstyle voicings to include more unfretted strings. The resulting chords are not only easier to play, but they are more colorful versions of the standard chords!

track 8

E	F#mi7(11)	G#mi7	A(add9)	B7	C#mi7

 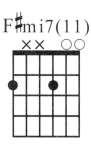 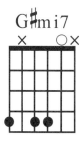  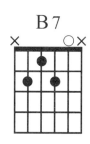 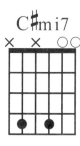

The additional voicings below can be used as alternatives for the chords directly above them.

E/G#	B7sus

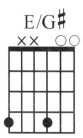 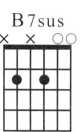

16

Exercises in the Key of E

Let's begin with the easiest exercise of them all. As promised, we will play the six main chords in the key of E with only two fingers on your left hand! The top staff of these exercises is written in music notation and directly below it is the same music written in tablature. Repeat these eight bar exercises until they feel comfortable, then go to the final chord in bar nine. It is best to practice them slowly, then increase the tempo as they become familiar to you. (Refer to page 13 for help with reading these symbols.)

track 9

The following exercise is the same as the exercise above, but instead of pausing between chord changes, it maintains a constant pattern.

track 10

17

The next two exercises are structured like the first two. In this exercise, there is a pause between chords to allow time to transition.

track 11

The following exercise uses the same pattern as the one above, but maintains a constant rhythm throughout.

track 12

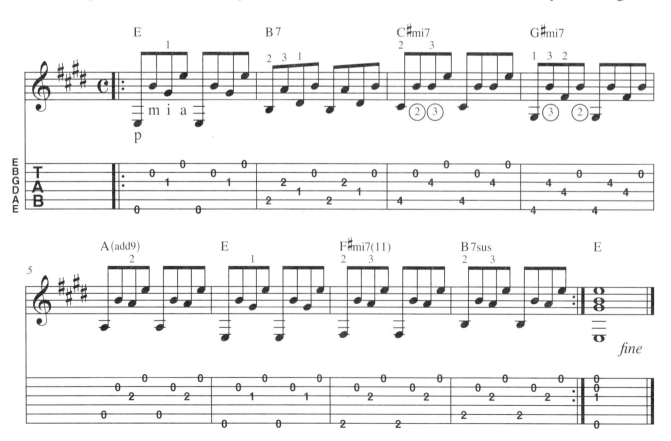

The left hand fingerings written above the notes are only suggestions, as there are many ways to finger these voicings. The fingerings selected are based on context—what was played before and what comes next—to minimize movement and smooth transitions.

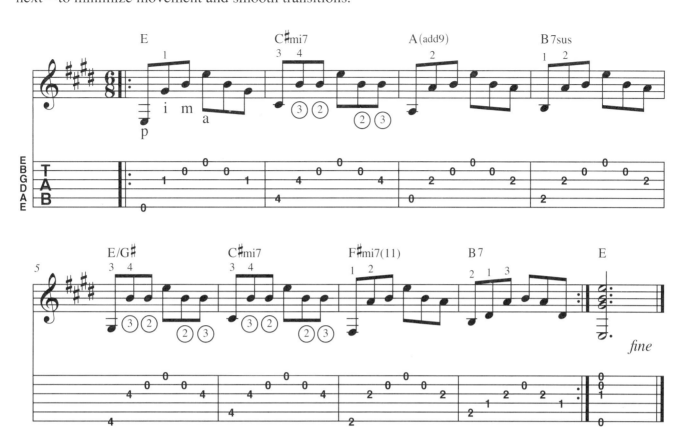

The exercise below is a common fingerstyle pattern often found in folk music. Beat 3 of each bar is not plucked to allow a break in the constant rhythm.

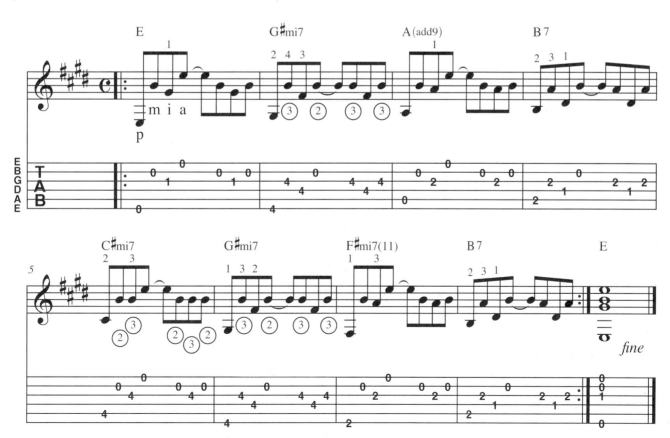

19

Key of A
Standard Guitar Voicings

The following chord graphs are standard guitar voicings of the six main chords in the key of A.

track 15

A	Bmi	C#mi	D	E7	F#mi

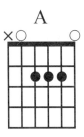 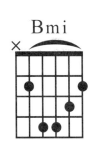 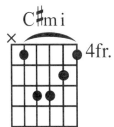 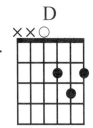 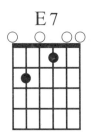 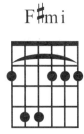

Open-String Fingerstyle Voicings

The chord graphs below are open-string fingerstyle voicings that can be used in place of the standard guitar voicings seen directly above each chord.

track 16

A(add9)	Bmi7(11)	C#mi7	D(add9)	E	F#mi7(11)

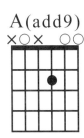 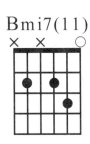 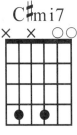 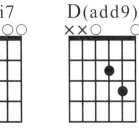 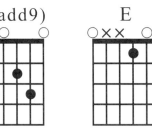 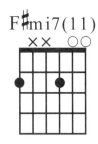

A(add9)/C#   *Additional voicings*   Esus

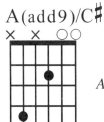 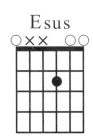

Exercises in the Key of A

The exercise patterns in the keys of A, D, G and C are similar to those established in the key of E. The chords, voicings, and fingerings vary to accommodate the different keys.

Remember to keep the fingers on your left hand curved and close to the fretboard. Press the strings with the tips of your fingers and make sure your thumb stays behind the neck.

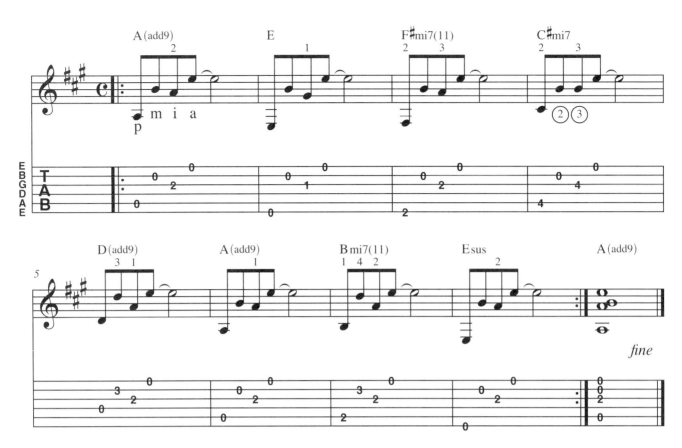

Plucking the strings at a slight diagonal will produce the best tone. Use the left sides of the fingernails on your right hand.

22

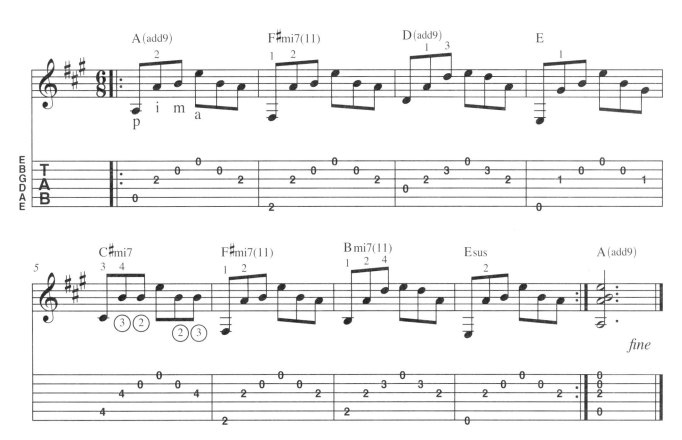

In bar 8 of the following exercise, the Esus chord resolves to an E chord on beat 4.

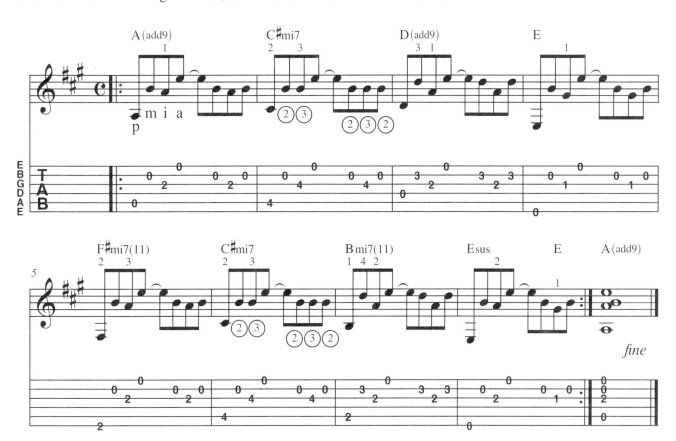

Key of D
Standard Guitar Voicings

The following chord graphs are standard guitar voicings of the six main chords in the key of D.

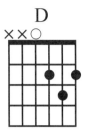 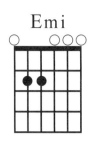  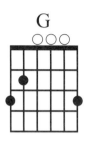 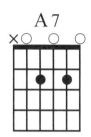 

Open-String Fingerstyle Voicings

The chord graphs below are open-string fingerstyle voicings that can be used in place of the standard guitar voicings seen directly above each chord.

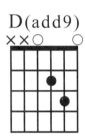 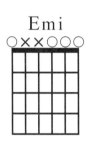 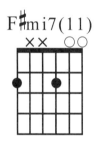  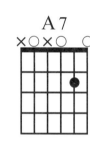 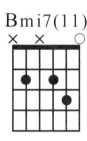

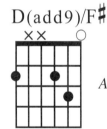 *Additional voicings*

Exercises in the Key of D

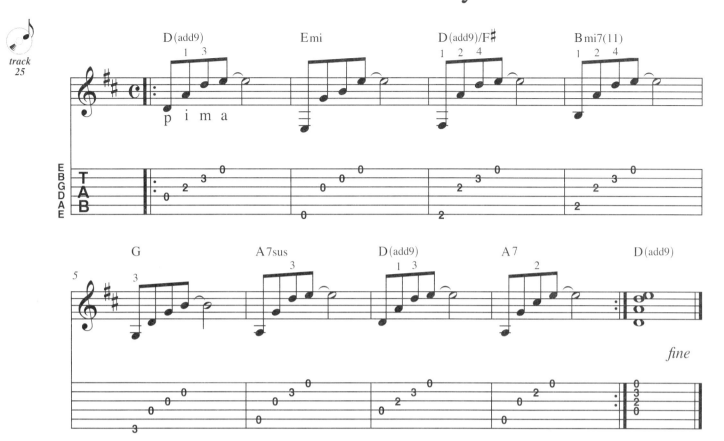

Listen carefully to the rhythm, volume and tone of the notes you are playing. Try to keep them as even and consistent as possible.

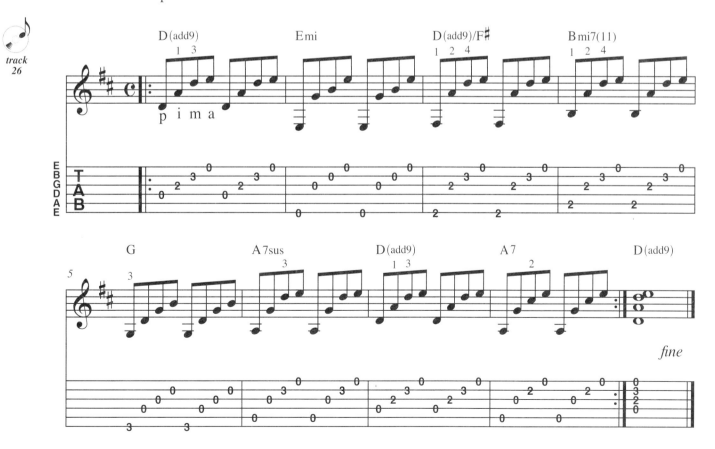

In the exercise below, the A(add9) chord in bar 2 has a different fingering from the A(add9) in bar 8. Though they are the same chord, they are preceded and followed by different chords; the suggested fingerings help to make the transitions as smooth and effortless as possible.

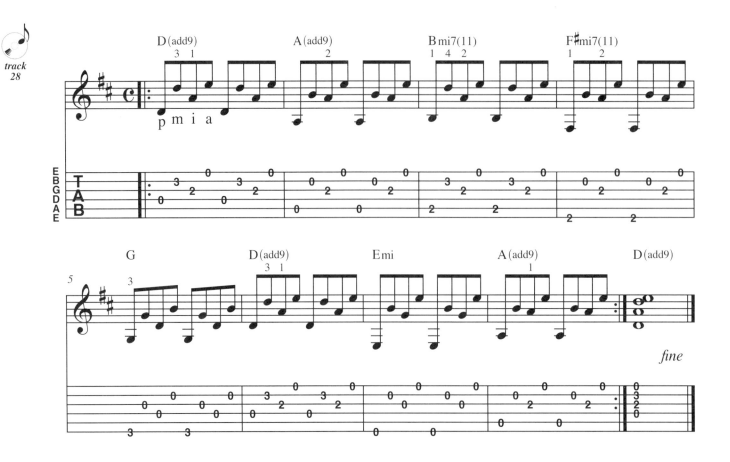

The first bar below presents another example of preparatory fingering. To change from the D(add9) chord to the Bmi7(11) chord in bar 2, you do not have to move your 2nd and 4th fingers.

Key of G
Standard Guitar Voicings

The following chord graphs are standard guitar voicings of the six main chords in the key of G.

track 31

G	Ami	Bmi	C	D7	Emi
	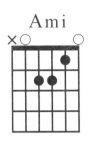		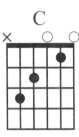	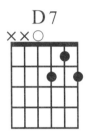	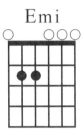

Open-String Fingerstyle Voicings

The chord graphs below are open-string fingerstyle voicings that can be used in place of the standard guitar voicings seen directly above each chord.

track 32

G	Ami7	Bmi7(11)	C(add9)	D(add9)	Emi
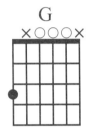		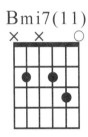			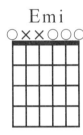

G/B	C/D
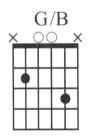	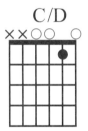

Additional voicings

Exercises in the Key of G

As in the key of E, you can play all the main chords in the key of G with only two fingers on your left hand! The following exercise demonstrates this incredibly simple progression.

In bars 4 and 5 of the next exercise, try sliding the 1st finger of your left hand from the 2nd fret to the 3rd fret of the A string. Sometimes sliding your fingers on the strings instead of lifting them off helps transitions sound more musical.

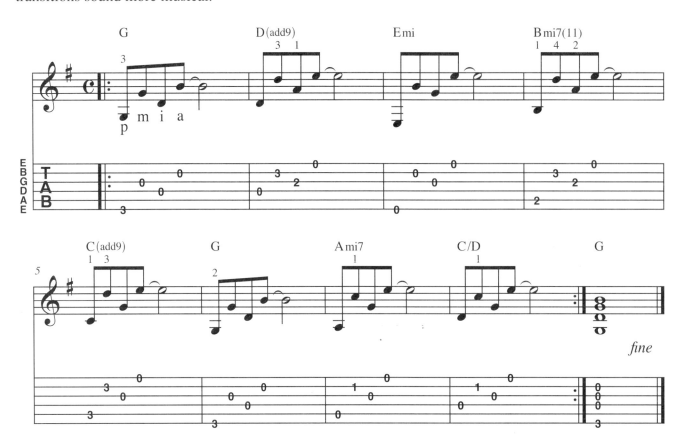

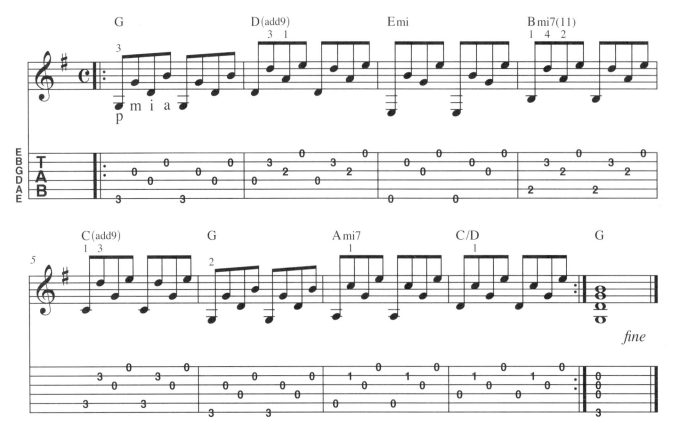

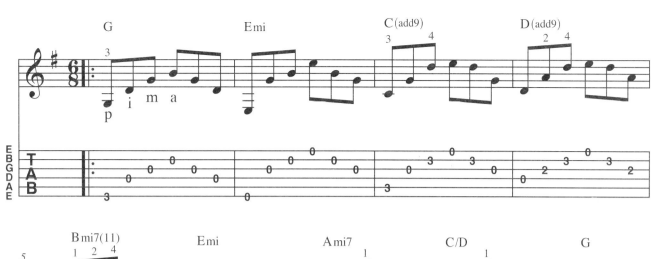

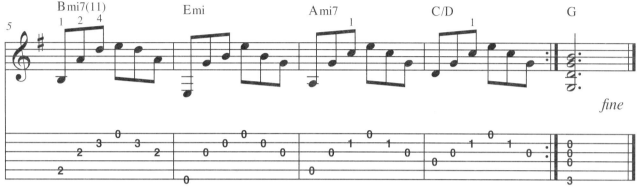

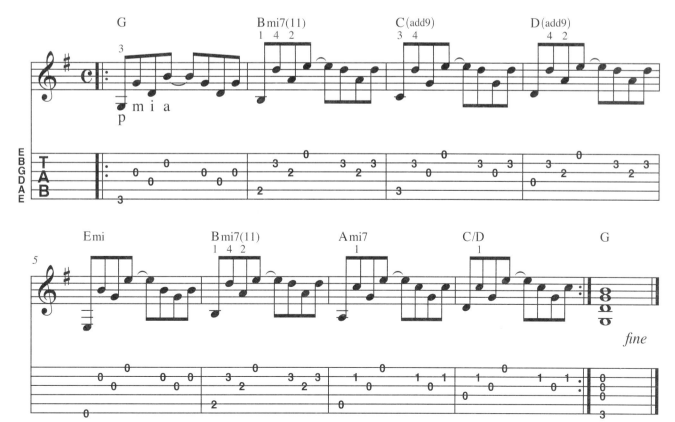

Key of C
Standard Guitar Voicings

The following chord graphs are standard guitar voicings of the six main chords in the key of C.

track 39

C	Dmi	Emi	F	G7	Ami
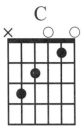				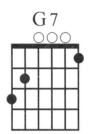	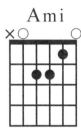

Open-String Fingerstyle Voicings

The chord graphs below are open-string fingerstyle voicings that can be used in place of the standard guitar voicings seen directly above each chord.

track 40

C(add9)	Dmi7	Emi	F	G7	Ami7
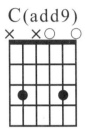		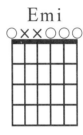		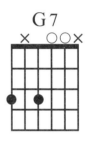	

Additional voicings

C/E	F(add9)	G
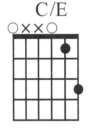		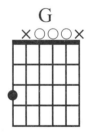

Gsus
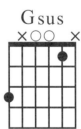

Exercises in the Key of C

To play the Dmi7 in measure 2 of this exercise, you must bar the 1st fret of the 1st and 2nd strings by flattening out your index finger over the two strings.

In bar 4 of the exercise below, use the 2nd finger of your left hand to prepare you for the F(add9) in bar 5; that way, you don't need to reposition this finger.

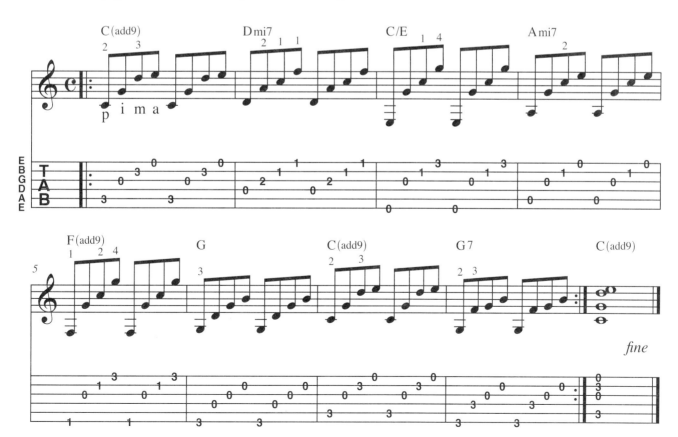

The F chord in measure 5 of the following exercise is the first instance of a full bar chord in these exercises. If you find it challenging to play, replace it with an F(add9) chord.

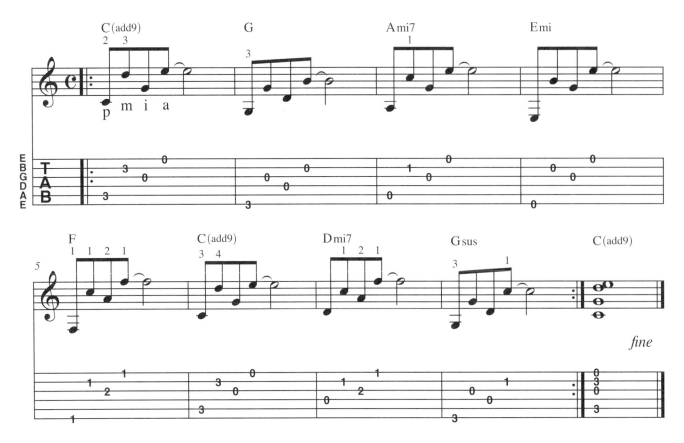

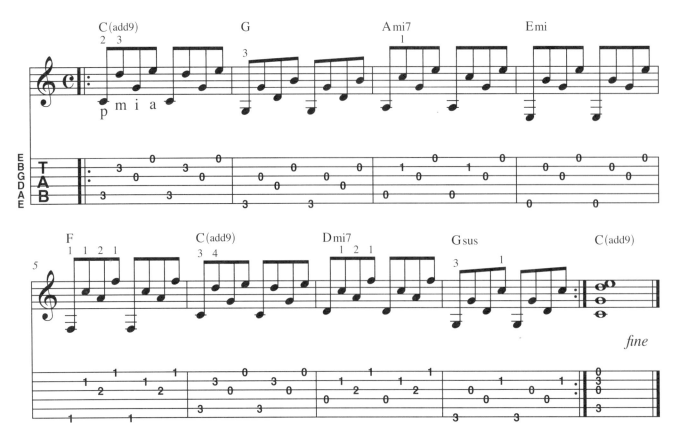

This last exercise introduces a resolution from Gsus to G in bar 8. The pattern is changed slightly to define this resolution on the upbeat of beat 3.

These exercises only cover a few fingerstyle patterns. The possibilities are endless. Try creating your own combinations of open-string fingerstyle voicings and experiment with different patterns.

Transposing with a Capo

Now that you have these exercises under your belt, let's learn how to play them in other keys. With the help of a capo, it's actually quite easy! A capo is used to raise the pitch of the open strings by clamping them down at a particular fret. Functionally, that fret becomes the nut of the guitar. For example, if you capo the 1st fret, the 2nd fret of the guitar becomes the 1st fret, the 3rd fret becomes the 2nd fret, and so on. As we mentioned earlier, the most common keys in guitar music are E, A, D, G, and C because they use the greatest number of open strings. A capo allows you to play the open-string fingerstyle voicings covered in this book in different keys.

Capo on 1st fret

Any key can be played by using a capo at many different fret positions. Open strings and voicings are primary considerations when choosing which fret to capo. We will explore the most basic positions of the capo at the 1st and 2nd frets. The images to the left and right show the capo at the 1st and 2nd frets respectively. Notice that the capo is clamped just behind the fret. This is the most effective placement of the capo to maintain intonation and prevent string buzz.

There are a total of twelve keys, and we covered five of them: E, A, D, G, and C.

Capo on 2nd fret

• The top row of the graph below lists the seven other keys we have not studied in this book. (A key in parenthesis indicates an enharmonic spelling, i.e., a different name for the same note or key. For example, A# is the enharmonic of Bb.)

• The second row, *Capo*, designates the placement of the capo.

• The third row, *Play Chords In*, refers to the key you play in to produce the new key listed at the top of that column. For example, to play in the key of F, you capo the 1st fret and play the open-string fingerstyle voicings in the key of E on page 16.

• The remaining six rows list the main chords of the new keys.

	Key of F	Key of Bb (or A#)	Key of Eb (or D#)	Key of Ab (or G#)	Key of Db (or C#)	Key of Gb (or F#)	Key of B
Capo	1st Fret	1st Fret	1st Fret	1st Fret	1st Fret	2nd Fret	2nd Fret
Play Chords In	E	A	D	G	C	E	A
1- major chord	F	Bb	Eb	Ab	Db	Gb	B
2 - minor chord	Gmi	Cmi	Fmi	Bbmi	Ebmi	Abmi	C#mi
3 - minor chord	Ami	Dmi	Gmi	Cmi	Fmi	Bbmi	D#mi
4 - major chord	Bb	Eb	Ab	Db	Gb	Cb	E
5 - major chord	C	F	Bb	Eb	Ab	Db	F#
6 - minor chord	Dmi	Gmi	Cmi	Fmi	Bbmi	Ebmi	G#mi

Congratulations! You are now able to play the six main chords in all twelve keys. You're well on your way to becoming a more knowledgeable and versatile guitarist!

The G Kilauea Tuning

The premise of the *Open-String Fingerstyle Method for Guitar* is to maximize the use of open strings to make fingerstyle playing easier and more beautiful. A more advanced application of this principle is to tune a guitar to different pitches to increase the number of open strings available.

For further study of the open-string approach, *Slack Key Guitar—The G Kilauea Tuning* book and CD present a tuning I have been using since 1998 for almost all of my fingerstyle playing. I have experimented with other tunings, and found the G Kilauea tuning to be the most versatile and functional for solo instrumentals and vocal accompaniment. Included in this instructional book are:

- Over 200 chords in the key of G

- Scales, thirds, and sixths in the key of G

- Six principles to help you create your own tunings

- Seven arrangement techniques for guitar

- Thirteen original compositions and arrangements of traditional Hawaiian songs presented in tablature and notation

- Audio CD of the thirteen original compositions and arrangements

Biography

From his simple beginnings in Honolulu to his life amid the hustle and bustle of Los Angeles, Daniel Ho has worked as a musician, producer, singer/songwriter, arranger, composer, engineer, and record company owner. The most compelling of these roles has been as a four-time GRAMMY® award-winning producer, featured slack key guitarist, and artist in the *Best Hawaiian Music Album* category.

Daniel's musical inclinations were apparent at an early age. His first instruments were organ and ‘ukulele, from which he graduated to classical guitar, piano, electric guitar, bass, drums, and eventually, voice. His passion for music led him to study composing, arranging and film scoring at the Grove School of Music in Los Angeles. He began his professional career as the leader, keyboardist, composer, and producer for *Kilauea*, a contemporary jazz group he formed in 1990. By 1997, *Kilauea* had released six chart-topping albums, two of which hit the Top 10 on Billboard's jazz charts.

As momentum of the smooth-jazz genre waned, Daniel set his sights on starting an independent record label. His interests in photography and graphic design complemented the requisite responsibilities of marketing and production. In 1998, he launched Daniel Ho Creations. Slowly, the releases grew into collaborative projects that featured *himeni* (Hawaiian hymnody), hula, ‘ukulele, and slack key guitar. To date, Daniel Ho Creations has released over seventy acoustic and Hawaiian-themed CDs by many of Hawai‘i's most respected artists, who are first and foremost friends. Daniel has received numerous Hawaiian music industry accolades including three *Na Hoku Hanohano* awards and ten *Hawai‘i Music Awards*.

In recent years, Daniel has been able to remain true to his craft and focus on what he loves most: the music. He is an accomplished singer and songwriter who has shared his music as a soloist throughout the U.S., Japan, Europe, and even Tasmania. He has been featured with the Honolulu Symphony; toured as a keyboardist and guitarist for GRAMMY® award-winning vocalist, Peabo Bryson; guest-lectured at Stanford University; and authored instructional books on music theory, ‘ukulele, and slack key guitar. On a behind-the-silver-screen note, he performed the Hawaiian-language cover of Prince's *Nothing Compares 2 U*, which can be heard during the end credits of the 2008 feature film *Forgetting Sarah Marshall*.

Also By Daniel Ho
Books

Discovering the ‘Ukulele	Herb Ohta, Jr. & D. Ho	Beginning instructional book
Exploring the ‘Ukulele	Herb Ohta, Jr. & D. Ho	Intermediate instructional book
Slack Key Guitar - the G Kilauea Tuning	D. Ho	Slack key instructional book
Got It!	Cindy Tseng & D. Ho	Beginning music theory book
Colorful Sounds	D. Ho	Advanced music theory book
Nā ‘ikena	Amy Stillman & D. Ho	Songbook of *‘ikena* & *He Nani* CDs
Pōlani	D. Ho	Solo ‘ukulele songbook of *Pōlani* CD

Selected Discography

Sunny Spaces	*‘ikena*	*Solo Slack Key - the G Kilauea Tuning*
Simple as a Sunrise	*He Nani*	*‘Ukuleles in Paradise*
Skies of Blue	*Watercolors*	*Step 2: ‘Ukuleles in Paradise 2*
Pōlani	*Harmony*	*2 to 3 Feet: ‘Ukuleles in Paradise 3*
KoAloha	*Mysteries*	*Hymns of Hawai‘i, vol. 1 & 2*
Pineapple Mango	*Paradise*	*Hawaiian Slack Key Guitar Collection*